THE ESSENTIAL HANDBOOK

The Sacristan
in the Church of England

Thomas J. D. Robertson

D1387346

kevin
mayhew

First published in Great Britain in 1992 by Kevin Mayhew Ltd
Buxhall, Stowmarket, Suffolk IP14 3BW
Tel: +44 (0) 1449 737978 Fax: +44 (0) 1449 737834
E-mail: info@kevinmayhewltd.com

www.kevinmayhew.com

9 8 7 6 5 4 3 OD

ISBN 978 0 86209 242 9
Catalogue No. 1425418

Cover design by Jonathan Stroulger
Illustrated by Graham Johnstone
Typeset by Veronica Ward

Printed and bound in Great Britain

CONTENTS

THE AUTHOR

Canon Robertson was formerly Vicar of Taddington, Chelmorton and Flagg, Derbyshire, and was also the Assistant Warden of the Readers' Board for the Derby Diocese. He has had considerable experience in parish work and also in teaching and lecturing.

FOREWORD

This book has been designed as an aid to those who have been appointed to undertake the work of sacristan in their church. Particularly in mind have been those in grouped parishes, sharing an incumbent, who have become involved for the first time in this work. In this secular age we need to remember that the sacred vessels and vestments of the Church are used to further God's Kingdom on earth. Sacristy work is a vital service to the Church; like every other aspect of church work, it is, surely, a privilege for the person concerned. The sacristan should never begin his or her work without a prayer of self-offering to God.

In the Anglican Communion there is a wide variety of eucharistic liturgical use, ranging from the plain to the ornate. In this book I have attempted to indicate a standard practice. Some readers may find this unsatisfactory, but I hope, nevertheless, they may find the book meets a need.

All the illustrations are 'typical' items to do with the work of a sacristan. Most churches have their own variations which may differ from those shown.

My indebtedness to many sources in compiling the book is clear. Any inaccuracies are entirely my own.

This manual is dedicated to all faithful sacristans of our churches in their devoted work.

THOMAS J D ROBERTSON

A Sacristan's Prayer

*O Lord, you have called me to serve you
in the Sanctuary of your Church.
Inspire me so to order all things
that our worship may reflect your holiness.
Bless all who minister at this altar;
all who receive here the holy Sacrament,
that we may grow in grace,
and become partakers of eternal life,
through Jesus Christ your Son, our Lord.*

T.J.D.R.

Chapter 1
THE SACRISTAN AND THE SACRISTY

A sacristan is a person appointed by a priest to care for the church's sacred vessels and vestments, and who prepares all the necessities for the service of Holy Communion (Eucharist).

Most of the preparatory work of the sacristan takes place in the sacristy. This has always been the room in a church for keeping the sacred vessels and the robes of the clergy, and the place where they rested. Introduced

The Sacristy Furniture

c.480 A.D. in Syria as an annexe to the apse, the sacristy had, by the Middle Ages, come to be built behind the high altar on the north or south side. In most churches today, however, it consists of a suite of rooms for clergy and lay servers, furnished with chests, cupboards, tables, liturgical books, vessels, a *prie-dieu* and a crucifix, and hand washing and toilet facilities. In early times it was used for the practice of Reservation of the Holy Sacrament. Today its use for this purpose is during the Holy Week ceremonies from Maundy Thursday to Holy Saturday. In current Anglican usage, where the room known as the 'clergy robe' may also be called the 'clergy or priest's vestry', 'sacristy' is applied to churches using elaborate ceremonial where large numbers of sacred objects have to be kept.

The Prie-dieu

The Sacristy should be separate from the choir vestry or the place where the churchwardens count the collection taken at services. The siting near the high altar reflects the practice of the old Roman basilica, which had the sacristy in this position so that processions could begin from the high altar, directly after robing.

This, then, is the room in which a fair part of the sacristan's work will be carried out. It is work which requires much care and devotion to detail – so much so that, in parishes where there is a daily Eucharist, it is helpful to have an assistant sacristan. Such assistance is invaluable during holiday periods. Indeed, large churches would benefit from having a team of sacristans, or deputies, to cover holidays or illness.

Sacristy Essentials

Within the sacristy, which should be carpeted, there should be a 'press' or 'chest' for storing the various sets of vestments used for the Eucharist. This consists of a specially constructed chest with a number of flat, shallow drawers in which each vestment set, together with its matching burse and veil (see pages 45 and 46), can be laid flat, with the minimum of folding. On the wall above the vestment press should hang a crucifix. If there is no vestment press available, then the vestments may be hung on clothes-hangers and hung in a suitable wardrobe. In this case, there should be a convenient table provided for laying out the vestments in preparation for the Eucharist. Otherwise, the top of the

The Vestment Press

vestment chest is always used for this purpose.

Other essentials for the sacristy include a basin, with running water if possible, and soap and towel for washing the hands, a reliable clock, and a long mirror to ensure the priestly robes are hanging correctly. Also, the altar book, or 'missal' and its rest, or 'cushion' are usually kept in the sacristy. (The Missal is used for the Eucharist; it contains the Holy Communion Service, together with Collects, Epistles and Gospels for the liturgical year.)

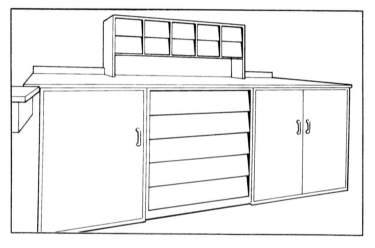

The sacristy should be furnished with a desk, or table, with pens, together with the parish Register of Services, and a current Church Lectionary (a booklet giving details of biblical readings for the services, and indicating the colour of vestments and altar frontals to be used according to the church season). There should also be a Diocesan Calendar or Year Book, which, besides giving necessary information, lists all parishes with their incumbents and assistant clergy to be prayed for in the daily intercessions. Appended to the Diocesan Calendar should be a card noting the name of the Diocesan Bishop, and those of the Suffragan or Assistant

Bishops. A small safe or cupboard will be essential for keeping the communion vessels and cruets.

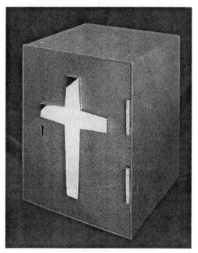

The Sacristy Safe

Cleanliness

Whatever arrangements are made for the cleaning of the church, the sacristan should keep the sacristy 'spick and span'. 'Cleanliness is next to godliness', and nowhere does this apply more than in the work of the sacristan, who should aim at a high standard of hygiene.

The need for care, in the light of AIDS, was emphasised in the following notice to all clergy issued in April 1987 by the Archbishops of Canterbury and York after consultation within the House of Bishops:

ARCHBISHOP'S NOTICE TO ALL CLERGY
CONCERNING CLEANLINESS

After discussion with the House of Bishops, we have decided to issue to all clergy the following guide about the use of the chalice:

Public concern about AIDS has aroused fears among some people that the sharing of the common cup might be a possible means of infection. The advice given to us by the highest medical authorities is that such fears are groundless. The virus which causes AIDS may occasionally be present in saliva, but recent research has shown that saliva inhibits the activity of the virus and that it has not been transmitted by being swallowed. There is therefore no reason to take special precautions when administering the chalice other than by application of the normal rules of hygiene listed below.

People who are infected by the virus or who have AIDS will be unusually susceptible to other infections and may wish, and should be allowed, to receive communion by intinction or in one kind.

Research on the chalice as a possible means of transmitting other types of infection has shown that the risk is extremely small. This can be reduced even further by observing the following rules:

1 A chalice of gold, silver or other suitable metal
   is to be preferred to pottery, particularly
   unglazed pottery.

2 The rim of the chalice should be firmly wiped
   with a purificator after it has left the lips of each
   communicant. The same part of the purificator
   should not be used repeatedly, nor should it be
   allowed to become sodden.

3 Anyone with cuts, sores or abrasions on their
   lips should receive intinction or in one kind.

4 In addition to ritual ablutions, the chalice should
   be thoroughly cleaned after use.

We suggest that this notice is displayed in the vestry or in some other suitable place within your church.

Robert Cantuar & John Ebor

Chapter 2
VESTMENTS & ROBES

Distinctive dress for various functions is worn in many professions. Not many have such a long history as church vestments, which are adaptations of classical costumes of the Roman Empire. As styles went out of fashion for everyday wear they were retained in church use with modifications.

The sacristan's duties involve caring for the eucharistic vestments, and laying out the appropriate set, according to the Church's season for each service. Where used, the sacred vestments for the priest are:

- Cassock
- Amice
- Alb
- Girdle
- Maniple (now unusual)
- Chasuble

The black surge *cassock* is the basic church attire of the priest, but in some churches today a *cassock-alb* has been introduced which obviates the need for cassock, amice, alb and girdle. In churches where priestly vestments are not worn, the surplice and stole of the appropriate colour are used for the Eucharist.

The Amice

Formerly a neck-cloth, the amice is a linen square with tapes attached to two corners, and is worn around the neck over the black cassock with the tapes fastening around the waist. When not in use, the amice is laid flat in a drawer of the vestment press.

The Alb

The alb is a long, white linen garment reaching to the ankles, derived from the ancient 'tunic', and worn over the priest's cassock and amice. Like the amice, some albs may have a piece of coloured material – an *apparel* – (the same colour as the vestment set for the prescribed season) attached at the foot, front and back. This enables them to hang evenly when worn.

When not in use, the alb is kept on a clothes-hanger, together with the girdle, in the cupboard.

The Girdle

The girdle is a woven length of white flax with tassels at both ends; it is fastened around the waist, over the alb, and looped inside the waistband at either side to hold the stole in position. Over a cassock-alb the stole may be worn hanging down loosely.

The girdle is hung with the alb in the cupboard when not in use.

The Maniple

The maniple is a narrow strip of material about 12-18 inches long, coloured to match the vestment set. It is looped at one end to fit over the priest's left arm, and has tassels at the other end. Originally, it served as a handkerchief. It is rarely used nowadays.

Maniples are laid flat in a drawer of the vestment press when not in use.

The Stole

The stole is a long length of material in the colour of the vestment set to which it belongs. A typical stole is $4\frac{1}{2}$ inches wide at the ends, tapering to 3 inches at the neck. It is worn around the priest's neck and hangs over his shoulders, over the alb and the amice. For the Eucharist, some priests may prefer the stole to be crossed at the waist with the tasselled ends inserted through loops made by the girdle. However, many priests today wear a cassock-alb and stole, in which case the stole measurements might be slightly wider than those given above.

When not in use, stoles are laid flat in a drawer of the vestment press.

The Chasuble

The chasuble is the outer garment of the sacred vestments. It is a length of material (coloured according to the church season) with an opening in the centre which is fitted over the priest's head, enabling both panels to fall back and front. Often worked into the material are the 'Y' shaped panels, or *orphreys*, symbolising the Cross.

When not is use the chasuble is housed in a drawer of the vestment press.

The Surplice

The surplice is a white, long-sleeved linen garment reaching to the knees, or just below, and gathered at the neck. Where vestments are not used, a surplice and coloured stole are worn for the Eucharist. The surplice is also worn surmounted by an academic hood for the Choir Offices of Matins and Evensong. It is also used by readers, choir members, and organist.

Surplices are kept on hangers in the cupboard when not in use.

The Cassock-alb

An increasingly popular modern vestment which may be worn instead of the traditional cassock, alb, amice, and chasuble is the cassock-alb. It is of white, mainly polyester, twill material and incorporates a sewn-on cowl. A girdle is usually worn around the waist.

When not in use, the cassock-alb should not be kept in the vestment press but hung on a hanger and placed in the cupboard.

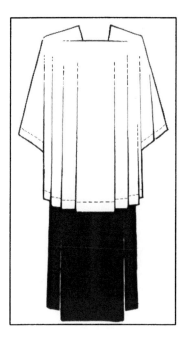

The Cotta

The cotta is similar in shape to the surplice but shorter, especially in the sleeves. It is chiefly worn by altar servers as an alternative to the surplice.

When not in use, the cotta is kept on a hanger in the cupboard.

The Cope

The cope, in the pre-Christian era, was simply a long cloak. It is a costly, embroidered vestment usually worn by priests in procession at festivals, and by Bishops for the sacraments of confirmation and ordination. It usually has *orphreys* on either side at the front, with a 'morse' (clasp) at the front for fastening. On the rear of the cope is hung a 'hood' in the shape of a shield, and some modern copes have the hood incorporated in the material. Copes are often worn with a matching stole.

The cope should be fitted over a large hanger and hung in the cupboard, when not in use.

The Academic Hood

The academic hood, signifying the priest's university or theological college, is worn over the surplice for the choir offices of matins and evensong with a black preaching scarf (see page 24).

The hood and scarf may be hung together on a peg in the cupboard.

The Black Scarf

The black scarf, broader than a stole, is worn around the priest's neck and hangs down over the academic hood for all Choir Offices.

How To Prepare The Vestments
For The Eucharist

1   As written, but not using the maniple and amice.

2   Lay the Stole on top of the Chasuble as (Greek Alphabet) letter A = alpha.

3   Lay the Girdle on top of the Stole as (Greek Alphabet) letter Ω = omega.

4   Lifting the front of the Chasuble covering the Stole and Girdle.

5   No's 2 to 7 N/A.

The Eucharistic Vestments

The eucharistic vestments are always kept in the vestment press, each coloured 'set' being placed in a separate drawer. The other robes are hung in the sacristy cupboard on hangers or pegs. The colour of the particular vestment set to be used is regulated by the Church Calendar (Lectionary) (see page 10), each church 'season' having its own distinctive colour: violet (purple) for Advent/Lent; white for Christmas/Easter, Trinity Sunday, Harvest and Dedication Festivals and certain Saints (e.g. B.V.M.); red for Pentecost (Whit Sunday) and Saints' days; and green for all 'ferial' Sundays after Pentecost (or after Trinity). These are all denoted in the Church Lectionary by their initial letters, V, W, R, G. The Lectionary is a necessary handbook for every sacristan (see page 10). Ferial days are 'ordinary' days – days that are non-festal or non-penitential.

HOW TO PREPARE THE VESTMENTS FOR THE EUCHARIST

1 Take the coloured *chasuble, stole, maniple* (all coloured according to church season), *amice* and *girdle* out of one of the vestment press drawers and lay the chasuble flat on top of the vestment chest with the rear side uppermost. Lift the bottom of the rear side and place on top of the neck of the chasuble.

2 Lay the coloured matching *stole* on top of the chasuble in the shape of the English capital 'H' vertically (actually, it is the capital long 'E' in the Greek alphabet).

3 Lay the *maniple* (if used) along the centre of the 'H' vertically. This represents the Greek capital 'I'.

4 Place the *girdle* over the stole forming it in the shape of the letter 'S'. Thus *stole, maniple* and *girdle* symbolise the first three letters of the Holy Name of Jesus (in Greek).

5 Spread the *alb* over the whole, folding the sleeves inwards at the sides, lifting up the rear and folding it at the top of the vestment chest.

6 Spread the *amice* on top of the *alb*, folding inwards the two sides and tapes towards the centre.

7 Cover the whole with a white dust cover.

HOW TO REPLACE THE VESTMENTS AFTER USE

1 Lay the *chasuble* flat on the vestment press with the rear uppermost.

2 Place on it the *stole* and *maniple* in the prescribed manner (see 2 and 3 above).

3 Lift up the rear and fold over till the bottom end touches the neck of the chasuble.

4 Turn inwards the right hand quarter, then the left.

5 Spread the *amice* over the whole, folding over the sides and tapes, and place in one of the vestment press drawers.

6 Hang the *alb* over a hanger and place in the cupboard together with the *girdle*.

Chapter 3
ALTAR LINEN

In many churches the 'Sewing Guild' or 'Linen Guild' care for the church linen, repairing and renewing the items as required. However, it is the sacristan who arranges the use of the altar linen for all communion services.

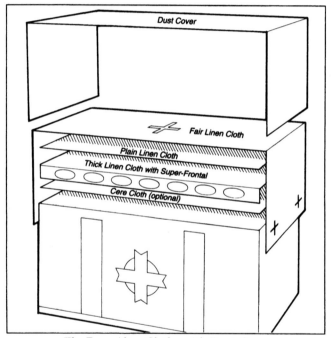

The Four Altar Cloths with Dust Cover

Five cloths may be used to cover the altar surface:

1 The *cere cloth*, next to the altar surface, has the primary function of preventing moisture from condensation dampening the linen cloths above it. Though useful in this way, the cloth is not always used nowadays.

2 The *super-frontal* (or *frontlet*) *cloth** is a thick linen cloth to which is stitched the silk, ornamental super-frontal. When in place, the super-frontal hangs down over the top of the altar frontal (see page 29). Its main purpose is to hide the hooks (or rod) on which the altar frontal hangs.

*In some churches, as an alternative to the super-frontal a fair linen cloth wider than the altar is used, the extra width hanging down over the altar frontal.

3 The *plain linen cloth*, whose dimensions are the same as those of the altar top, is placed on top of the *super-frontal*.

4 Next comes the *fair linen cloth* – a cloth of very fine linen, the same width as the altar top, but falling down on each side to within a few inches of the floor. It has five woven crosses, one at its centre and one at each corner.

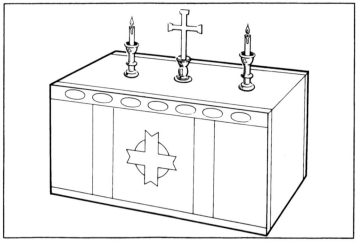

The Altar with Dust Cover in position

5 The *dust cover*, of coarse material, is used to cover and protect the other cloths.

Some altars may be left uncovered when not in use, especially central or nave altars.

Altar Frontals

Altar frontals in rich embroidered materials, coloured according to the church's seasons, may be hung in front of the altar. The super-frontal covers the rod, or hooks, from which the altar frontal is suspended to a depth of 7-10 inches, and covers the top of the altar frontal.

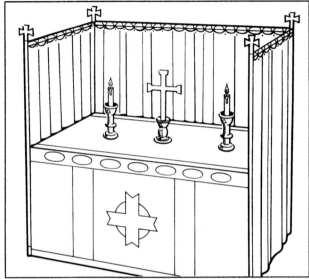

The 'English' Altar

Altar Curtains

If the high altar is of the 'English' type, with riddel posts, curtains will hang on the north and south sides, and a 'dorsal' curtain at the rear instead of a *reredos* (an ornamental screen covering the wall at the back of the altar). These curtains, also, are in the care of the sacristan. They are always of the same colour as the altar frontal and will, therefore, be changed when the frontal is changed according to the church season. The curtains hang from brass rods fitted into slots at the top corner of each post. When changed, they should be neatly folded and kept in a chest for curtains and other accessories, separate from the frontals chest.

HOW TO PREPARE THE ALTAR
FOR THE EUCHARIST

1 If the altar frontal has to be changed, remove the altar cross and candles, then the dust cover, the fair linen cloth and the plain linen cloth. Take off the super-frontal cloth, then unhook the altar frontal, placing them both in the *altar frontals chest* – a chest the same width and height as the altar, fitted with horizontal laths which slip into grooves at each side. (This chest may be kept at any convenient place within the body of the church.) The frontals are hung over these laths.

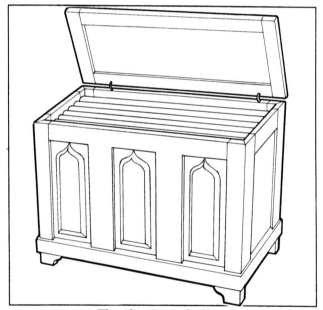

The Altar Frontals Chest

2 Remove the replacement frontal and super-frontal from the frontals chest and hang the frontal by its sewn-on rings to the hooks at the top in front of the altar (or, if used, from a brass or wooden pole inserted through loops at the top of the frontal).

3 Lay the super-frontal cloth on top of the cere cloth, if used, so that the ornamental super-frontal hangs down over the top of the altar frontal.

4 Lay the plain linen cloth over the super-frontal cloth.

5 Lay the fair linen cloth over the plain cloth, checking that it hangs equally on both sides.

6 Replace the altar cross and candles.

7 Place the altar cushion, or rest, with the altar book (Missal) at the epistle side of the altar.

8 (If the priest desires this) remove the compacted (built-up) chalice from the sacristy. Take the corporal out of the burse (see pages 46 and 47), spreading it centrally in front of the altar cross, and place the burse to the rear on the gospel side. Place the veiled compacted chalice (see page 45) on the corporal, pulling the front corners of the veil to the edge of the corporal, left and right.

9 Remove from the sacristy the glass tray with the cruets, wafer-box, lavabo jug, bowl and towel, and place on the credence table. These items are described in later chapters.

AFTER THE SERVICE

1 Remove the cross and candles, and spread the dust cover over the altar. Replace the cross and candlesticks.

2 Remove the glass tray from the credence table to the sacristy.

Note on Laundering

The fair linen cloth should be carefully steam ironed, spotless, and without crease. It is best preserved in this way after ironing by placing it on a wooden roller, on which it is rolled up as it is being ironed. The fair linen cloth should be changed every two or three months, and the plain linen cloth three times a year. Wine stains can be removed during laundering by placing the stained part of the cloth in boiling milk.

Chapter 4
THE CRUETS & CREDENCE TABLE

The cruets for holding wine and water at the Eucharist are usually of clear crystal or glass, though other materials may be used. When not in use they should stand in an oblong glass dish, or on a glass strip laid on a table in the sacristy. When in use they are placed on the linen cloth on the table known as the credence, or credence table, which stands on the south side of the sanctuary.

The Wine & Water Cruets - Silver and Glass

Together with the two cruets for wine and water, there should be a glass bowl and jug of water, and, laid alongside, a folded strip of hemmed linen known as the 'lavabo' towel – a towel required for the ritual of the priest cleansing his fingers at the offertory (see page 51).

Also on the credence table, between the two cruets, is laid the wafer-box, of wood or metal. The interior of the box is divided into sections, into which the wafers may be fitted.

The Wafer Box

The sacristan, in the vestry preparing for the service, places the required number of wafers in the wafer-box, wine and water in each of the cruets and water in the jug within the bowl for the lavabo. These, together with the lavabo towel, are placed on the glass tray or dish in the sacristy. This is then removed to the credence table.

The Credence Table

The Altar Cushion

Then the altar book or 'Missal', on its cushion or rest, is removed and placed on the epistle (south) side of the altar, open at the Collect, Epistle and Gospel for the day.

Unfortunately, it is no longer safe to leave the vessels on the credence table after services, or within the credence cupboard (a cupboard built into some credence tables). All must be removed to the sacristy safe after use, for secure keeping. If the church is ancient there will be a credence built into the south wall of the sanctuary, with an adjacent *piscina* – a shallow basin cut into the stone with a hole in its centre into which the remains of the water blessed by the priest was poured during the 'ablutions' after the communion of the people. The *piscina* served as a drain which emptied directly into consecrated ground outside.

It is convenient, where there is no *piscina* in the sanctuary, for one to be fitted in the sacristy. Where this is not possible, a basin should be provided and kept exclusively for this purpose, being emptied into clean earth as soon as possible after the service.

To avoid incrustation on the inside of the glass cruets, they should be rinsed out after service and turned upside-down on the glass tray to drain. Persistent stains on the glass may be removed with tea leaves and water, briskly shaken, or salt and water, or a denture tablet dissolved in water. When dry, they should be wiped with a clean linen towel and replaced in the sacristy safe with the communion vessels.

Altar Book Rest in Wood and Brass

Chapter 5
SILVERWARE

In preparing for the Eucharist, the sacristan will need to remove the communion vessels from the locked safe in the sacristy (or vestry). If the vessels are of silver they do not need cleaning with silver polish very often (and never on the inside), provided they are washed regularly and wiped with a soft tea-cloth. When silver polish is used, however, always wash it afterwards with very hot water and a small drop of washing-up liquid, and rinse away the soap. Unless this is done thoroughly, especially with the chalice, traces of silver polish may react with the wine to produce an unpleasant taste; even the slightest trace of polish can be detected. Further, the wine tends to 'hold' in small patches on the inside of the chalice when the priest administers it, unless the washing process has been thoroughly done. Another difficulty concerns the lipsticks used by some women, which tend to build up on the outer rim of the chalice, making regular cleansing and cleaning essential.

The sacred vessels are:

- Paten
- Chalice
- Ciborium
- Pyx
- Flagon (where used)
- Monstrance (where used)

These vessels are made of silver, or gold, and the inner sides are usually gilt.

Important: Silver polish must never be used on the inside of a gilt-washed chalice. Such vessels should be cleansed in ordinary washing-up liquid.

The Paten

The paten is a circular silver plate for holding the priest's wafer, or, where there is no ciborium (see page 40), for holding both priest's and people's wafers. It may have a concave, smooth base or, more usually, a shallow recessed base, so that it fits exactly over the rim of the chalice. As silver is a soft metal which quickly scratches and wears, the sacristan should never place silver upon silver without a purificator (a special cloth) between them (see pages 50 and 53). The purificator is laid across the mouth of the chalice, and the paten placed on top of it.

The Paten

The Chalice

The Chalice

While the cup of the chalice holding the communion wine must always be perfectly plain and smooth, a cross, or another sacred Christian symbol, may be engraved on the foot of the chalice to mark the side from which it is administered. The base may also be studded with jewels, so the chalice needs careful handling as these are sometimes displaced with rubbing or if the chalice is knocked over.

The Ciborium

The ciborium, which holds the people's wafers, is similar in shape to the chalice but usually smaller. It has a cover or lid surmounted by a small cross. This vessel should be handled with particular care for the cross or the lid may be bent, or even knocked off, if mishandled or dropped on the floor. Nowadays, the ciborium is generally used instead of the paten for public communion as the ciborium gives greater convenience and safety in administering.

The Ciborium

For notes on how to prepare the sacred vessels in the sacristy for the Eucharist (see pages 52 and 53).

Note on Eucharistic Bread

In the Eucharistic rite most Eastern churches use leavened bread, while the Western churches use unleavened bread. 'Best wheaten bread, such as is used to be eaten, whether loaf bread or wafer', is the term prescribed in the 1662 Prayer Book. Wafer bread was enjoined in the 1549 Prayer Book, 'unleavened and round'. This was substituted in the 1552 Book, but reintroduced in 1662. In the Canons of 1969, it is stated that bread, whether leavened or unleavened, 'shall be of the best and purest wheat flour'. Wafer bread has obvious advantages: absence of crumbs, and convenience of administration to each individual communicant. The wine may be a port or sherry type and the Canons of 1969 state that this should be 'the fermented juice of the grape, good and wholesome'. Some churches prefer to use a non-alcoholic wine.

The Pyx

The pyx is a much smaller silver circular box, hinged at one side so that the cover acts as a lid. This vessel holds the 'reserved', intincted wafers for placing in the *aumbry* – a closed recess in the wall which is usually veiled by a curtain when not in use (see page 42). Rarely, and where permitted, a *tabernacle* (box) on the altar may be used instead of an aumbrey. The pyx is used for taking communion to the sick at home or in hospital, or the infirm or elderly who are unable to attend church. It is usually kept in a silk-lined bag attached to which are

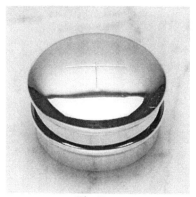

The Pyx

cords, so that it can be hung from the priest's neck and suspended on the chest where it is tucked under the crossed stole.

The Aumbry

Note on Intinction

Intinction is the practice of lightly dipping the wafers in the consecrated wine in the chalice, though some priests reserve the sacrament without intincting the wafers.

The Flagon

In festival celebrations of the Eucharist where there are a larger than usual number of communicants, a flagon may be used; part filled with wine it is placed on the credence table to provide a further supply, if needed, of communion wine. The flagon is a large silver jug, but with a hinged, fitted lid to ensure the sacred wine is always covered. Some cathedrals and churches consecrate extra wine in the flagon and use it to refill the chalice as numbers require. In this case, the flagon is placed on the altar at the offertory with its lid open.

The Monstrance

In some churches a monstrance may be used. It is made of silver, similar in shape to a pyx, but adorned with decorative or symbolic representations. It consists mainly of a spherical frame of gold or silver rays in the centre of which is a receptacle *(lunette)* with a glass window through which the consecrated host (wafer) may be seen. It is used in the devotion of 'Benediction'. During the 'exposition' point in the devotion the sacred host is removed from the tabernacle or aumbry, placed in the *lunette* and held at eye-level by the officiating priest, who turns to bless the congregation while the *Tantum ergo* is sung. When placed on the altar the monstrance is covered by a white veil.

Chapter 6
LINEN FOR THE EUCHARIST

The Chalice Veil

The chalice veil should be of soft silk in the colour of the vestment set to which it belongs, in size about 21 inches square. A cross in gold or silk thread is embroidered in the centre, near the edge. It is lined with silk, or similar quality material. The chalice veil is used to cover the chalice and paten. It is removed during the service at the offertory and placed flat on the epistle side, the back edge being brought forward and turned back, and the front edge folded on top, with the cross showing. The veil is replaced after the people's communion and the ablutions. The paten is replaced on the chalice, and the

The Chalice Veil
(in position covering 'compacted' chalice with burse on top)

veil is placed over these vessels, the cross on the veil being at the front, centre; the corners of the veil are pulled lightly to the front of the corporal, left and right. The chalice and veil are moved to the right, and the corporal is folded and placed in the burse (see pages 46 and 47). This is laid on top of the chalice veil in the way shown above.

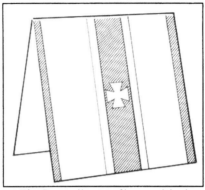

The Burse (in standing position)

The Burse

The burse is a case of two pieces of cardboard, each about 9 inches square, hinged on one side. The two squares are covered with material matching the chalice veil and the vestment set to which it belongs. They may then be sewn with strong thread along the hinge. The two squares are lined on the inside with white linen. One of the two squares is embroidered on the outside with a cross in the centre in gold or silk thread. The burse houses the corporal, and also the pall (see page 49), when those cloths are not in use.

In preparing for the communion service the corporal is removed from the burse and spread in the centre of the altar in front of the altar cross, and the veiled chalice and paten are placed upon it. The burse is then placed to the left, on the gospel side to the rear of the chalice, standing open with the hinge at the top and the side with the embroidered cross facing front (see page 45).

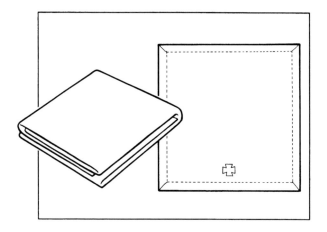

The Corporal

The corporal is a white linen hemmed cloth about 18-20 inches square. It takes its name from the Latin *corpus, corporis* meaning 'body', and is the cloth upon which the consecration of the bread and wine takes place. It is always marked with a small cross embroidered near the hem in the centre of the side nearest the priest when he stands in the centre before the altar. In laundering, the corporal should be steam-ironed and folded in a special way:

1 Fold the corporal into three by turning the front portion marked with the cross over towards the middle, then lifting the rear portion towards the middle and folding it on top of the first fold.

2 Again, fold the cloth in three by turning the left-hand [Right] side over towards the middle, and bringing the right [Left] hand side towards the middle to lie on top of the first fold.

47

The Corporal – Folding Method

This method of folding ensures that the central portion of the cloth is preserved unsoiled when not in use. At the end of a service it is always folded in this way by the priest and placed in the burse, which is then put on top of the veiled chalice and paten, with the opening of the burse to the right. It is carried in this way to the sacristy. It is kept in the vestment chest, together with the veil, in the drawer containing the vestment set of the same colour.

The Chalice with Purificator (see page 50) and Pall in place.

The Pall

The pall is a stiff, fine white linen-covered square of about 6 inches which is used for covering the paten, and also the chalice during the administration. It consists of two folds of linen sewn together but open at one end, into which a stiff piece of cardboard cut to size, can be inserted. The top side of this 'case' may be embroidered with a threaded cross in the centre. If the two pieces of linen are lightly stitched, the under-piece can always be detached and replaced with a new square of linen when the original square becomes badly soiled. The pall is placed on top of the paten holding the priest's wafer, and during the actual service, when the administration of the consecrated wine takes place, the pall is used to cover the chalice.

After service the pall is kept inside the burse with the corporal and placed in one of the drawers of the vestment press. Palls need frequent inspection as they tend to be stained from the rim of the chalice when covered during communion.

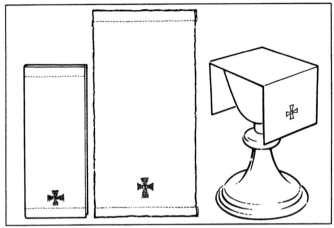

The Lavabo Towel & Purificator

The Purificator

The purificator is a cloth of medium quality linen used for wiping the chalice during and after its use. Its size is about 15 inches by 9 inches, or any size to suit convenience and the chalice in use. It is folded first lengthwise in three, and then again in three so that the centre square may lie over the cup of the chalice with the two ends hanging over the edge of the chalice on either side. The cloth carries a small embroidered cross centred at one end.

After use, the soiled purificator should be left to soak in a glass bowl of water in the sacristy. Later, it may be taken to be laundered. A clean purificator is used for every communion service. A simple towel rail or rack fixed to the wall of the sacristy is a useful addition. The sacristan may hang the soaked purificators on the rail to dry before laundering.

The Lavabo Towel

This towel is of medium quality linen, in size about 24 inches by 12 inches. It has an embroidered cross which should be visible above the hem in the bottom of the central panel after the towel has been folded lengthwise in three folds. The Lavabo towel is placed on the credence table by the side of the glass bowl and jug. The towel is used for drying the priest's fingers at the offertory, before he proceeds to the consecration.

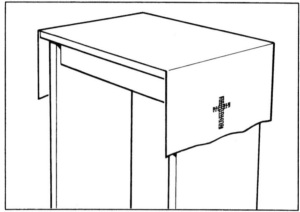

The Credence Table ready for use

Credence Table Linen

The top of the credence table should be covered first with a length of coarse cloth, coloured rep, or billiard cloth, cut to the size of the table top. Next is placed over it a linen cloth, fitted so as to hang down a few inches at the sides, and slightly extended over the front and back. When not in use this is covered by a coarse linen dust cover, large enough to hang over and completely cover the linen, or left bare.

HOW TO PREPARE THE SACRED VESSELS IN THE SACRISTY FOR THE EUCHARIST

1 Place the *chalice* (p.39) on the table.

2 Place a folded *purificator* (p.50) across the rim of the chalice.

3 Place the *paten* (p.39) on top of the purificator, fitting it on to the chalice.

4 Place a priest's host (wafer) on the paten.

5 Place a *pall* (p.49) on the paten, covering the host.

6 Place the *chalice veil* (p.45), coloured to match the vestments of the season, over the pall. Turn up the near side of the veil and bring it up to lay it back on top of the pall with the lining showing, enabling the priest to hold the chalice in his hand.

7 Place a folded *corporal* (p.47) within the *burse* (p.46).

8 Place the *burse* on top of the veil covering the chalice with the opening to the right.

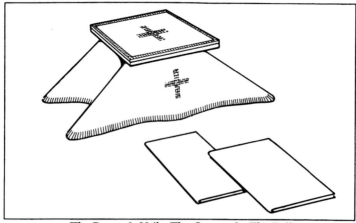

The Burse & Veil   The Corporal   The Pall

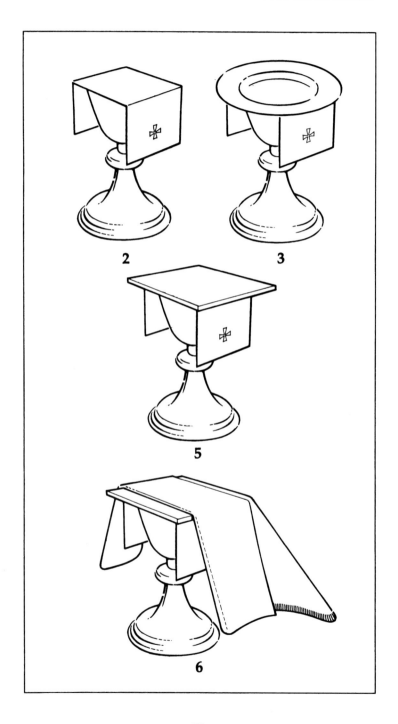

2   3

5

6

Some priests may allow the sacristan to 'lay the table' on the day of the service. The sacristan would then remove the built-up (compacted) chalice and burse and veil to the altar, spread the corporal, place the burse near the candlestick(s) on the north side, place the veiled chalice in the centre of the corporal and adjust the fall of the veil. He would then remove the glass tray with cruets containing wine and water, and the filled wafer-box to the credence table, followed by the lavabo bowl, and jug (with water) and the lavabo towel (see page 51).

Chapter 7
ALTAR CANDLES

Traditionally, candles have been used in celebrating the Eucharist since the early days of Christian worship in the Roman catacombs. Symbolically, their use is taken to represent Christ as 'the light of the world', and the use of two candles in Anglican worship to symbolise the two natures of Christ – divine and human.

The Altar Cross & Candles
with top covers

The provision and care of the altar candles is part of the work of the sacristan (unless directed otherwise by the incumbent). Altar candles should contain 65% beeswax, and tallow – animal fat – may not be used. Wax candles improve by being kept in store for a few months, so the sacristan need not be concerned about ordering a large quantity for storage in the sacristy chest. When dirty they can be cleaned with a cloth dampened in turpentine. When the burning down of altar candles makes an appreciable difference to their height, it is desirable to replace them with new ones. This should be done not only out of reverence for the Blessed Sacrament, but also to avoid a low-burning candle guttering the socket of the candlestick causing the wax to overflow with the danger of soiling the fair linen altar cloth. If this should happen, the fair linen cloth should always be washed. If there is no time for this, cover the stain with a piece of blotting paper and use a warm iron, or a 'stain remover'; this will usually remove the wax. If wax has been spilled on the sanctuary or chancel carpet during the Gospel, or other procession, by the carrying of acolytes' candlesticks, it may be removed by placing brown paper over the wax spot to absorb the grease and applying a warm iron (or use a 'stain remover').

To control the downward flow of wax during burning, porcelain covers may be used to fit over the top of the candle. When the candle has burnt low the cover may be lifted off and fitted over the top of the new replacement candle.

For funerals and requiems candles of brown or unbleached wax are often used, and these should be ordered and stored by the sacristan.

In preparing the altar for the Eucharist the sacristan (if there is no server) will light the candles beginning at the epistle side, and then the gospel side. In extinguishing them at the end of the service, the reverse order is used.

Chapter 8
LAMPS, INCENSE & HOLY OILS

In parish churches where the Blessed Sacrament is 'reserved' in an aumbry in a side-chapel, a lamp is required to burn in close proximity to the aumbry. It should remain alight 'day and night perpetually'. The supervision of the lamp, and the provision of pure olive oil and the wick is usually undertaken by the sacristan. The bowl should be of uncoloured glass 'to give a white light', according to the rubrics. It signifies the presence of the Lord in the Sacrament reserved in a pyx within the aumbry. When the light has to be extinguished for the renewal of the wick or oil, or for the cleaning of the bowl, a lighted candle is lit from the lamp and placed in position. After cleaning, refilling and inserting a new wick, the lamp is re-lit from the candle. The lamp is hung from a bracket above the aumbry door. Alternatively, an eight-day type of candle may be used in the bowl instead of the oil and wick.

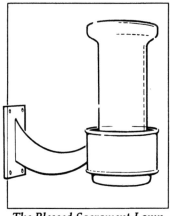

The Blessed Sacrament Lamp

The Sanctuary Lamp

Similarly, a lamp may hang over the sanctuary, but here a coloured glass bowl is used with oil and wick, it need not be kept continually alight. For these lights, many churches use a low voltage light bulb, wired from a suitable adjacent power socket.

Incense

Incense has for centuries been used in celebrations of the Holy Eucharist. The smoke is said to represent the prayer of the faithful. In the Western Church its use has largely been confined to solemn sung Eucharistic rites, but since 1969 it has been permitted at any Eucharist. In the Church of England its use is associated with the Anglo-Catholic movement, and in those parishes which favour that tradition.

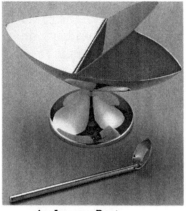

An Incense Boat
(with spoon for grains)

The Incense Thurible

Although the sacred vessels connected with the use of incense are usually supervised by the Master of Ceremonies, or Senior Server, the task may be undertaken by the sacristan. This will involve the ordering of incense grains and charcoal, and the regular cleaning of the incense boat and thurible (or censer). As these are mainly of electroplated nickel silver, EPNS, only careful washing and drying with a soft cloth are necessary. Incidentally, servers need careful instruction and plenty of private practice before being placed in charge of the thurible.

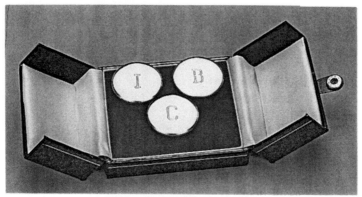

Three Single Holy Oil Stocks

I = Oleum Infirmiorum (for the sick)
B = Oleum Catechumenorum (for Baptism)
C = Chrisma (for Confirmation and Consecration)

Holy Oils

The holy oils used for anointing the sick, for baptisms, and for confirmation, for blessing the font on Holy Saturday, and for other consecrations are consecrated by the Bishop in his cathedral at the Eucharist on Maundy Thursday. The oils are kept in holy oil stocks which are placed in the sacristy safe or in some other lockable safe place. The old oils left over from the previous year should be used for burning in the blessed sacrament lamp hanging above the aumbry.

ECCLESIASTICAL SUPPLIERS

It is the sacristan's duty to order fresh supplies of wine and wafers, candles, and incense (where used). Many of the items featured can be obtained from the publisher.

For our latest, free catalogue or for further information or other stockists' details, please contact:

Kevin Mayhew Limited
Buxhall, Stowmarket
Suffolk IP14 3BW

Telephone 01449 737978
Fax 01449 737834
E-mail info@kevinmayhewltd.com

NOTES

NOTES

NOTES

NOTES

Lightning Source UK Ltd.
Milton Keynes UK
UKOW05f2243230813

215904UK00001B/6/P

9 780862 092429